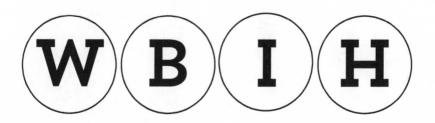

T0163885

WE BELONG
IN HISTORY

WRITING WITH
WILLIAM STAFFORD

Ooligan Press | Portland, Oregon

We Belong in History: Writing with William Stafford
© 2013 Ooligan Press

ISBN13: 978-1-932010-68-8

Cover Design: Lorna Nakell
Interior Design: Adam Salazar

Acknowledgments:

Anushka N.'s "Someone Walks by Rocky Waters," first appeared in *Ink-Filled Page* (2010).

William Stafford's poems, "Ceremony," "Fall Wind," "Parentage," "Representing Far Places," "Traveling Through the Dark," and "Vocation," were first collected in *Traveling Through the Dark* (Harper & Row, 1962).*

William Stafford's poems, "Level Light," "Listening," and "The Well Rising," were first collected in *West of Your City* (Talisman Press, 1960).*

William Stafford's essay, "A Way of Writing," was first published in the journal *Field* in 1970. It also appears in *Writing the Australian Crawl* (University of Michigan Press, 1978).*

*Permission granted by Graywolf Press to reprint these poems and essay by William Stafford.

Printed in the United States of America

Publisher certification awarded by Green Press Initiative

www.greenpressinitiative.org

CONTENTS

WRITING WITH WILLIAM STAFFORD ON NATURE

WRITING WITH WILLIAM STAFFORD ON FAMILY

WRITING WITH WILLIAM STAFFORD ON MOMENTS IN TIME

WRITING WITH WILLIAM STAFFORD LESSON PLANS

PUBLISHER'S NOTE

At Ooligan Press, we live in Oregon and work with books. For anyone in the literary world in this upper left corner of the country, William Stafford's presence is all around. If you went to school in Oregon, you most likely read some of Stafford's poems or essays. And lucky you, because as you'll see in this book, his words and ideas are inspiring and thought provoking, opening new ideas, new worlds, new emotions.

When planning for the Stafford centennial birthday celebrations started in 2012, we started thinking about how we could be at the party, too. Since we make books, it made sense to go that direction. It also made sense to involve students, since part of our mission as a publisher is to involve classrooms in the publishing process because we believe that publishing is a great, but underused, tool for teaching literacy and the love of words. And so we hatched a plan for a state-wide writing contest calling on middle and high school students and their teachers to bring William Stafford's works into their literary lives.

To facilitate the contest, two wonderful Oregon teachers wrote engaging lesson plans for language arts teachers. We have to thank Erin Fox Ocón and Robin Scialabba for their willingness to share their passion for teaching, poetry, and the intersection of the two. These lesson plans are included at the end of the book in hopes that they will inspire teachers around the world to pull William Stafford into their own classrooms. Some teachers participating in the contest used these lesson plans, and, some used their own ideas. Either way, the idea was simple: use William Stafford's words to inspire the next generation of writers and poets.

Teachers and students from around the state—Eagle Point, Portland, Corbett, and beyond—participated and responded to Stafford's work. The very best of the entries we received are collected in this volume, *We Belong in History: Writing with William Stafford*. The writers range in age from sixth to twelfth graders, and they have written poems that fall into three loose categories: Nature, Family, and Moments in Time. Each section of this book is introduced by three poems by William Stafford, some of the same poems the students used to write their original pieces.

In addition to poetry, we have included Stafford's essay, "A Way of Writing." As every schoolkid has discovered, the writing process unfolds differently for each of us. Stafford's description of the writing process is his own, but it is a far cry from a prevailing idea that words leap from pen (or fingertips) to page (or screen) in great pure and meaningful bouts of genius. Instead he presents a cerebral and playful description of his own writing process, one full of hard work, but also full of passion and enjoyment and play.

We like to imagine that William Stafford would be excited to work with the students in this book. We like to think that he would like to stand up next to these students and read poetry with them. We like to believe that the work in this book connects us all to this larger-than-life literary figure from the plains of Kansas and the hills of Oregon. We are proud to offer this collection to the collection of Stafford works out there and hope that its publication will inspire others to write along with William Stafford.

—Ooligan Press

THE WILLIAM STAFFORD CLASSROOM

PAULANN PETERSEN

> *"There isn't really such a room with a connection*
> *to this struggling poet—is there?"*

These are the words of a famous writer. They're the opening sentence of a letter dated 23 March 1993, a letter I'd just received from Bill Stafford, that "struggling poet" extraordinaire. He was asking about my classroom at West Linn High School.

I was in the spring of my second year at West Linn, a markedly crowded high school facility. The first year I taught there, my classroom was an AV cart I pushed to a different place each period, using other teachers' rooms during their prep times. The second year, I got a classroom of my own, and the privilege of naming it. The West Linn English Department had a Jane Austen Room, a William Shakespeare Room, a Robert Frost Room, and a number of other rooms named—by the teachers who occupied them—for major literary figures.

It was my turn. What writer did I want to honor? I was a teacher who wrote, a writer who taught. What better writer/teacher/luminary than Bill? What better star than the one shining close to home, in Lake Oswego, just a few miles north of West Linn? So, the brass plaque above the door leading into my newly acquired classroom said *THE WILLIAM STAFFORD ROOM*.

By that spring of 1993, I'd had several months to settle in. On one wall, I'd put a number of Bill's poems and photographs of him. But he wasn't the only person feted in that room. On other walls, I'd posted my students' poems and dozens of photographs they'd taken. I put up student paintings and drawings I'd purchased. And big posters of Jimi Hendrix, Billie Holiday, Bob Marley, Tina Turner, and Miles Davis. And programs from West Linn theatrical productions. Then more posters of Janis Joplin, Thelonious Monk, Grace Slick, John Lee Hooker, Dexter Gordon, and Judith Jamison. The room buzzed with color and pizzazz. I'd painted a wild sunburst on the wall, surrounding the clock. Thai kites flew up and around the fluorescent lights.

I wanted to celebrate this showcase of creative personalities, so I wrote to Bill asking if he'd be willing to preside at a dedication party. In my letter to him, I briefly described the room, naming some of the others honored there, wondering if he'd be put off by such an eclectic, unconventional bunch.

He wasn't. He agreed to come.

The late April dedication day was stormy and raw. I filled the room with bouquets of lilacs from home. The department teachers pitched in to provide cookies and punch. An hour before Bill was due, the power went out. As soon as my last class left, I scrambled—pushing the refreshment table up near the room's only outside window, hoping that its bit of natural light would be enough for Bill to read the few poems he'd said he'd read, enough to spotlight him. But why did I bother to worry? The power came back on shortly after Bill arrived.

People gathered in the room—teachers and students, a few with requests. Anne, our Fulbright Exchange teacher from Australia, asked him to read "Fifteen," a poem she'd taught for years down under. She was astonished that this world-famous poet had come to visit. A National Book Award winner, a former US Poet Laureate was right there in the American public high school where she'd been assigned. She couldn't quite believe it. Neither could the rest of us. We were gathered to dedicate a room named for a poet and peace activist who was extraordinarily dedicated to our community of readers and writers and teachers. We had come to honor him. By being there—in his easy, unassuming way—Bill was honoring us.

Bill read the poems people requested. He talked with our students, our teachers. He signed books, even putting his signature below "Fifteen" where it appeared in the text book Anne had brought with her. The afternoon grew late. Bill took his leave.

That day I'd brought a pot of Stargazer lilies to school, a gift for him to take home to Dorothy, a small way of saying thanks. Standing in my classroom doorway, under the WILLIAM STAFFORD ROOM plaque, I watched him walk away—down the long hall, toward the outside door. He had the pot of lilies in his right arm, tucked up against his ribs. With each step, those pale blooms bobbed from side to side.

That was April. He died in August.

Later, after the memorial gathering for Bill at Lewis & Clark, Kim Stafford and I exchanged a few words about the dedication of that classroom at West Linn High. I told Kim I was still a little amazed that his father would take the time and trouble to be there that late April afternoon. Amazed at his unpretentiousness. Grateful for his generosity to other teachers.

"Oh," Kim said, "That's just like Daddy! He was such a small-town guy."

That small-town guy has now been gone for twenty years. But not really. Bill Stafford's poems—his voice and vision—are as alive as ever.

That West Linn High School classroom I named for him has been gone for close to fifteen years—demolished to make way for a new high school structure. But not really. The William Stafford Classroom lives wherever teachers invite Bill's poems into the spaces they share with their students.

And now we have a book designed to help teachers invite Bill's poems into a classroom, a book filled with the kind of student essays and poems that can result from such an invitation. *We Belong in History: Writing with William Stafford*. What a fine title. What a fine and potent notion: Bill's words as the inspiration for student writing.

In Bill's poems we find a voice that invites us to do our own adventuring in literature. His is a voice that invites us into "...rooms in a life, apart from others, rich/with whatever happens..." This is a voice of accessibility, telling us that poems can be as near as the very center of our lives. Poetry isn't the domain of the select, the elect. Poetry is, as Bill Stafford assures us, the domain of anyone willing to listen, anyone willing to watch for all that the wide world sends swirling our way. Poetry is the domain of students in classrooms everywhere. There are few poets more hospitable to other writers than Bill. A Stafford poem is a perfect springboard for generating student writing.

2014 is the William Stafford Centennial Year. Bill would have turned one hundred on January 17, 2014. People in Oregon, in Kansas, in places all over America, in spots all over this world, will gather to honor him, to celebrate his work. Some of those celebrations will be big. Some will be gala. Some will feature famous folks who will have come to pay tribute to Bill. Those occasions will be grand. And I'm looking forward to being part of the audience at some of them.

But most of all, I relish the thought of smaller gatherings, ones that are classroom sized. A teacher and her students. A teacher and his students. A group of learners gathered to see where writing can take them. A group ready to take one of Bill's poems as a starting place, as the best of places to begin.

A WAY OF WRITING

WILLIAM STAFFORD | *Composed 1969, Published 1970*

A writer is not so much someone who has something to say as he is someone who has found a process that will bring about new things he would not have thought of if he had not started to say them. That is, he does not draw on a reservoir; instead, he engages in an activity that brings to him a whole succession of unforeseen stories, poems, essays, plays, laws, philosophies, religions, or—but wait!

Back in school, from the first when I began to try to write things, I felt this richness. One thing would lead to another; the world would give and give. Now, after twenty years or so of trying, I live by that certain richness, an idea hard to pin, difficult to say, and perhaps offensive to some. For there are strange implications in it.

One implication is the importance of just plain receptivity. When I write, I like to have an interval before me when I am not likely to be interrupted. For me, this means usually the early morning, before others are awake. I get pen and paper, take a glance out of the window (often it is dark out there), and wait. It is like fishing. But I do not wait very long, for there is always a nibble—and this is where receptivity comes in. To get started I will accept anything that occurs to me. Something always occurs, of course, to any of us. We can't keep from thinking. Maybe I have to settle for an immediate impression: it's cold, or hot, or dark, or bright, or in between! Or well, the possibilities are endless. If I put down something, that thing will help the next thing come, and I'm off. If I let the process go on, things will occur to me that were not at all in my mind when I started. These things, odd or trivial as they may be, are somehow connected. And if I let them string out, surprising things will happen.

If I let them string out.... Along with initial receptivity, then, there is another readiness: I must be willing to fail. If I am to keep on writing, I cannot bother to insist on high standards. I must get into action and not let anything stop me, or even slow me much. By "standards" I do not mean "correctness" spelling, punctuation, and so on. These details become mechanical for anyone who writes for a while. I am thinking about such matters as social significance, positive values, consistency, etc.... I resolutely disregard these. Something better, greater, is happening! I am following a process that leads so wildly and originally into new territory that no judgment can at the moment be made about values, significance, and so on. I am making something new, something that has not been judged before. Later others—and maybe I myself—will make judgments. Now, I am headlong to discover. Any distraction may harm the creating.

So, receptive, careless of failure, I spin out things on the page. And a wonderful freedom comes. If something occurs to me, it is all right to accept it. It has one justification: it occurs to me. No one else can guide me. I must follow my own weak, wandering, diffident impulses.

A strange bonus happens. At times, without my insisting on it, my writings become coherent; the successive elements that occur to me are clearly related. They lead by themselves to new connections. Sometimes the language, even the syllables that happen along, may start a trend. Sometimes the materials alert me to something waiting in my mind, ready for sustained attention. At such times, I allow myself to be eloquent, or intentional, or for great swoops (Treacherous! Not to be trusted!) reasonable. But I do not insist on any of that; for I know that back of my activity there will be the coherence of myself, and that indulgence of my impulses will bring recurrent patterns and meanings again.

This attitude toward the process of writing creatively suggests a problem for me, in terms of what others say. They talk about "skills" in writing. Without denying that I do have experience, wide reading, automatic orthodoxies and maneuvers of various kinds, I still must insist that I am often baffled about what "skill" has to do with the precious little area of confusion when I do not know what I am going to say and then I find out what I am going to say. That precious interval I am unable to bridge by skill. What can I witness about it? It remains mysterious, just as all of us must feel puzzled about how we are so inventive as to be able to talk along through complexities with our friends, not needing to plan what we are going to say, but never stalled for long in our confident forward progress. Skill? If so, it is the skill we all have, something we must have learned before the age of three or four.

A writer is one who has become accustomed to trusting that grace, or luck, or—skill.

Yet another attitude I find necessary: most of what I write, like most of what I say in casual conversation, will not amount to much. Even I will realize, and even at the time, that it is not negotiable. It will be like practice. In conversation I allow myself random remarks—in fact, as I recall, that is the way I learned to talk—so in writing I launch many expendable efforts. A result of this free way of writing is that I am not writing for others, mostly; they will not see the product at all unless the activity eventuates in something that later appears to be worthy. My guide is the self, and its adventuring in the language brings about communication.

This process-rather-than-substance view of writing invites a final, dual reflection:

Writers may not be special or talented in any usual sense. They are simply engaged in sustained use of a language skill we all have. Their "creations" come about through confident reliance on stray impulses that will, with trust, find occasional patterns that are satisfying.

But writing itself is one of the great, free human activities. There is scope for individuality, and elation, and discovery, in writing. For the person who follows with trust and forgiveness what occurs to him, the world remains always ready and deep, an inexhaustible environment, with the combined vividness of an actuality and flexibility of a dream. Working back and forth between experience and thought, writers have more than space and time can offer. They have the whole unexplored realm of human vision.

THE POWER OF A POEM

WHEN YOU READ a good poem, it's like opening your eyes for the first time. It gives you a moment of poignancy. It changes you, for better or for worse, and never leaves you the same way as you were before. It gives you a precise joy, yet leaves you wandering into the mysteries you will never solve. There is no exact good poem or bad poem. The beauty is in the eye of the beholder, making you feel you are the only one that understands.

When I write a poem, I want to feel the enjoyment the reader does. I distance myself from my body and let my hand take over.... The difference is astounding when using a model poem. When you write, you seem to filter your thoughts, thinking, "does this relate?" When you alter your thoughts, you understand what a gift poetry is.

—ANUSHKA N.

WE BELONG IN HISTORY

REFLECTIONS ON WRITING

*"I write only because / there is a voice within
me / that will not be stilled."*

–SYLVIA PLATH

WHEN I WAS a child I thought everyone wrote poetry. The pencil that I gripped was not special and did not create miracles or any special sort of phenomena. There were just thousands of words that stayed safe in my journals in the dark drawer next to my bed. It wasn't until I was older that I realized I was capable of doing what other people weren't—and even later to actually own my ability. The passion I have for writing is something I can't explain nor do I wish to. There is only one way to put it and that is the swift, curious wonder I have for the world and my desire to document it. I can take out my notebook and write down the findings of the world I am in. I can analyze my messy brain, characterize how someone made me feel, fictionalize how I wish it was, and contemplate opinions, ideas and values, all with the art of writing. I can write my own rules, balance stanzas in ways no one else has, decide not to label it "poetry" or "memoir" but something exactly in between. As a writer, one is never fully a master of the art, but a student until the very end. There is so much to learn, and I can't wait to learn it. There is a voice within me, as Plath says, and I don't want it to be stilled.

—KIAH B.

WRITING WITH WILLIAM STAFFORD ON NATURE

FALL WIND

WILLIAM STAFFORD | *Composed 1956, Published 1962*

Pods of summer crowd around the door;
I take them in the autumn of my hands.

Last night I heard the first cold wind outside;
the wind blew soft, and yet I shiver twice:

Once for thin walls, once for the sound of time.

CEREMONY

WILLIAM STAFFORD | *Composed 1956, Published 1960*

On the third finger of my left hand
under the bank of the Ninnescah
a muskrat whirled and bit to the bone.
The mangled hand made the water red.

That was something the ocean would remember:
I saw me in the current flowing through the land,
rolling, touching roots, the world incarnadined,
and the river richer by a kind of marriage.

While in the woods an owl started quavering
with drops like tears I raised my arm.
Under the bank a muskrat was trembling
with meaning my hand would wear forever.

In that river my blood flowed on.

LEVEL LIGHT

WILLIAM STAFFORD | *Composed 1955, Published 1960*

Sometimes the light when evening fails
stains all haystacked country and hills,
runs the cornrows and clasps the barn
with that kind of color escaped from corn
that brings to autumn the winter word—
a level shaft that tells the world:

> *It is too late now for earlier ways;*
> *now there are only some other ways,*
> *and only one way to find them—fail.*

In one stride night then takes the hill.

HELPERS

CATHERINE M.

We are the bark that hugs the sturdy trees,
Like warm blankets we embrace
Over cold cracks and crevices.
Honeyed dew sticks
Cleansing tough skin,
Dampening morning air,
Air we are able to breathe.
The white globe swings, with dents
Like Swiss cheese, always watching us,
Shooting crystal balls of light that give the world
Life.
We are here, stuck to
One being as thick as ropes of licorice
Sticky with sap and sweet with creation.

PRIDE

ALEXANDER H.

The eagle stands tall and proud,
Swooping majestically;
King of the skies,
Sits upon his unannounced throne,

All-seeing from his perch,
Most important of them all,
Arrogant and self-important;
Once freed from the cage,
He realizes
He is not the biggest of them all.

SPRING

CLAIRE B.

I bounce on the hard cold ground.
On every step, the plants quiver and stand up tall.
They shake and sputter getting rid of the icy cold that
Has made them dormant for so long.
But now they are up swaying in the
Warm soft wind
That I blow on them.
The animals small and large slowly emerge from their dens,
Stretching their tender arms and legs.
They blink rapidly because of the change of light.
I sprinkle soft smiling rain on them,
A welcoming,
A gift.
They had passed the bitter and unforgiving winter,
"Welcome to spring" I whisper through the wind and pass the
    ray of sun.

SLOWLY FREEZING

AUDREY B.

The cool, brisk air
Stings my face
As the leaves fall in slow motion.
It is the time of light blankets of frost
Shrouding fields of grass.
The time of gathering up the leaves
Into tall, wide, mountainous piles.
The flowers cannot withstand the cold
And retire for a few months.
It is as if everything is slowly
Stopping. Ending. Halting its process
Until spring gives them hope.

THE AGE OF WINTER

OLIVER K.

The days of youth were always of a summer day.
I could play in the fruity fields and bathe in the warm, crispy,
    heat.
I would do whatever I wanted to do. I was free.

But now I'm imprisoned.
Everything is so cold.
Everything is so wet.
Everything is so cloudy.
It feels as if the age of winter will never end.

THE WHIP OF ICE

Dylan P.

The frost of winds
cracks its whip against
an oak door,
and the thunder of
ice shatters the
swirl of snow-laden clouds,
knocking loose the starlight
of its cold cargo.

SPRING

Spring is the crown jewel of the seasons.
Wearing its verdant, green robes, studded with crystal droplets
    of iridescent dew.
Lord of the four seasons, Spring wears a radiant halo of blazing
    petals.
It drifts through the fragrant air,
Inspiring the birds to chirp,
And giving flowers the resolve to erupt into bloom.
Spring is gentle rains, and all things that grow.
The sun shines on spring.

FOURTH

Julia R.

tonight:
the sharp sweet opening to—
something, or so I whispered to my palms
they glowed electric with heat and melted ice cream under
    fracturing artificial stars
every year in July, we burn fissures across the sky.

above me,
chemists shattered the same color wheels that those founders,
    those fathers, saw
in the slow blurry turn of countries, of men:
rainbows shuttering themselves from the sun,
universes shattering in shades and scales
if you can breathe long enough to stop seeing the burned ground.

LIGHTNING STRIKE

AMELIA W.

Strike once—strike again.
One hits the rod—the others hit the ground.
Crackle from above;
I hit trees with force.
Next comes the thunder;
it booms to signify its presence.
A storm is here.
Rain begins to fall;
I flash, splitting off into separate strikes.
This continues until the rain begins to slow,
and the thunder begins to space out.
The storm is moving on,
so I do too, traveling to places unknown,
leaving few traces of my arrival or departure.

LAST DAY OF SUMMER

ELLA D.

I climb the tree,
Rough bark scraping my hands.
I sit on my favorite branch,
And stare out
Into the wilderness,
The crook in the branch
Hugging my waist.
Feeling the autumn breeze
Against my face,
Pushing back my hair.
I breathe in the summer wind
For the last time,
Then autumn comes.

BURDEN OF THE SPIDERS

COLWYN J.

Terribly misunderstood
Because of its relatives
The spider, always hated and feared
Like a little drop of water, floating down from the ceiling
With eight spindly legs, and eight tiny eyes that look like small
    drops of oil
Hated, but always optimistic
Just like humans

Always keeping the pests in check
The spider represents humility
Always humble and ready to hide

EQUINOX

Ruby N.

Around the edge of a broken tree,
I watched as the sunlight began to grow through the hushed
    dawn
Quieting winter

Through the ice and dirt that crunches under my feet,
Silence that falls through waking limbs of trees

The sudden cold of forgotten sunlight, the wind blew soft,
yet I shiver twice

Once for my fading winter, once for the coming spring

CEREMONY

CLAIRA C.

On the shores of an evening sea,
I whisper goodbye to
midnight sun coming over the setting moon,
turning the sky red.

I drop a skipping stone in a slow-moving river:
the ripples whirl downstream
and get lost in the current.

Over the field a star glows;
black bats bathed in sunlight swoop
around trembling leaves,
around trees,
and the forest.

I stand on the banks of a morning river,
I see the midday moon over
a rising star,
and the sky is blue.

FIRE

SAM S.

Like a child,
who climbs a tree,
scratching bark off
with every step,
it sits within the branches,
reaching for the apples
with arms just barely
too short.
It wraps its legs
around the branches,
while extending its body
up the tree
using the tips of its fingers.
It inches closer to the red fruit,
now able to see its own reflection,
but still out of reach.
It finally makes one last lunge for the apple.
Time is a white noise,
a treasure
unused by anything,
but the living.

SOMEONE WALKS BY ROCKY WATERS

ANUSHKA N.

Someone walks by
those rocky waters thinking, going
into one self, seeing the stream
race without matter or thought,
up and down, utterly happy.

Those by the rocky waters
throw stones and watch
waves, not caring if
someone is better than
another.

Just knowing
who, what, why, where,
when everything
happened. Knowing what
matters and what doesn't.

Just being in that
space that you can
think freely.

Just there.

REFLECTIONS ON WRITING

IF THERE'S ONE thing I've learned about writing, it's that risk is inevitable and vital. You have to put your ideas, your experiences, and your voice out there, even when it is terrifying.

—JULIA R.

WRITING WITH WILLIAM STAFFORD
ON FAMILY

LISTENING

WILLIAM STAFFORD | *Composed 1952, Published 1960*

My father could hear a little animal step,
or a moth in the dark against the screen,
and every far sound called the listening out
into places where the rest of us had never been.

More spoke to him from the soft wild night
than came to our porch for us on the wind;
we would watch him look up and his face go keen
till the walls of the world flared, widened.

My father heard so much that we still stand
inviting the quiet by turning the face,
waiting for a time when something in the night
will touch us too from that other place.

PARENTAGE

WILLIAM STAFFORD | *Composed 1955, Published 1962*

My father didn't really belong in history.
He kept looking over his shoulder at some mistake.
He was a stranger to me, for I belong.

There never was a particular he couldn't understand,
but there were too many in too long a row,
and like many another he was overwhelmed.

Today drinking coffee I look over the cup
and want to have the right amount of fear,
preferring to be saved and not, like him, heroic.

I want to be as afraid as the teeth are big,
I want to be as dumb as the wise are wrong:
I'd just as soon be pushed by events to where I belong.

VOCATION

William Stafford | *Composed 1961, Published 1962*

This dream the world is having about itself
includes a trace on the plains of the Oregon trail,
a groove in the grass my father showed us all
one day while meadow larks were trying to tell
something better about to happen.

I dreamed the trace to the mountains, over the hills,
and there a girl who belonged wherever she was.
But then my mother called us back to the car:
she was afraid; she always blamed the place,
the time, anything my father planned.

Now both of my parents, the long line through the plain,
the meadowlarks, the sky, the world's whole dream
remain, and I hear him say while I stand between the two,
helpless, both of them part of me:
"Your job is to find what the world is trying to be."

RAIN

KYRA M.

When rain hits our house, we open the doors and windows.
Not because we want to give up and just let it flood in, but
because we don't hide from it. Instead we follow her.

She leads us under her cover of experience. A mother and a best
friend. Her fondest memories of our first appearance in life,
and her greatest fear that she see one of us end.

It took her time to realize the value of knowledge, this is what
she regrets. She tries to teach us from her past and tells us
whatever we dream, we can get.

CAN YOU HEAR THE BEAT?

COREY B.

If the world is listening you surely can hear,
The beat of her heart so loving, so near.
Through the bruises, through the chemo,
It still beats.
The heart of a fighter ready to stand.

Her determination still burns bright,
The cross-country march for everyone's right.
The bombs stand still as she makes her move,
Saving the world one step at a time.

Three kids through the schools,
Playing around, being fools.
Through their mistakes, the beat still strong,
helping them live so very long.

If the world is listening it would be deafening.
The beat.
The sound that changed my life.
The sound that stopped the bombs.
The sound of my mom's heart, so strong.

THE WOMAN I CALL GRANDMA

Lauren G.

If the world is listening, then come and see
the beautiful sight that is my grandmother.

Feel her thin, achromatic hair,
laying even on her head, without a stray to be found.

Smell her subtle, aromatic scent that fills the air,
when she spritzes it with perfume, soaking it up like a sponge.

If the world is listening, come and try
her tantalizing food, dancing on your tongue.

See her hover over the stove,
taking all day to make a homemade dinner.

Taste the mouthwatering meals together she wove,
cranking out apple cores for her fresh, frozen, fruity applesauce.

If the world is listening, come and observe
the astonishing fairytale-like castle she calls home.

Crane your neck to see the vibrant stained glass
displaying grapes molded into her windows.

Sit on my grandma's dew-dripping grass
and pluck the crimson colored raspberries from their vines.

If the world is listening, come and hear
of my wonderful grandma, Marjorie Peters.

Watch her drive to church every Sunday morning,
filling in the squares of the crossword puzzles after.

Feel her velvety hand hold yours.

Feel her kiss the top of your head, clinging onto the memory,
not letting it crumble away in your fingertips.

If the world is listening, come and remember
all of the recollections of times you spent with someone you
	treasured.

Come and see the beautiful, youthful caring woman I call
Grandma.

CEREMONY

DREW F.

My mind whirled
As I looked up
At the mangled arms of my relatives dancing

No one knew me
And I knew no one
But somehow these people are connected,
Jointed by the bone

A hand touched my hair
Sweat dripped
The ground swallowed all the sound

The rhythm of the Ninnescah
Bounced off the walls

My mind whirled
As I was pulled into their dance

FOUND IN THE DARK

ZACK T.

Lost in the dark, I couldn't find my family.
It is usually best to wait for them:
that situation is fragile, to leave and swerve might make more
    lost.

By glow of the street lamp I waited for someone I knew
and counted the moths next to the bulb, flickering, old as the
    road:
about to go out any second.

I waited longer, but it had been a while.
My eyes watching people gave me discomfort—
their faces cold.

I stood in the rain as it made the sidewalk slippery.
Around myself I could tell
nobody was worried.

I thought hard for discovery—my only swerving
I saw my mother; that pushed her over the edge.

I AM FROM OREGON

Anushka N.

I am from Oregon
where the raindrops drip,
tending to trees my age.

I am from fir trees, no sun, and fun days.
I am from sitting under blossom trees
Just for the feeling.

I am from the snowy days,
peaceful as a white blanket over mother life.
I am from nature, bookworms and cold construction.

I am from pilgrims who brought apples.
I am from the leaders who lead revolutions without fear.
Today is another day I am alive.

YOUTH

Catherine M.

When I closed my eyes,
Surrounded by rushing
Streams mopped dry at the sides
With prickly grass and mud,
The sun shone bright.
I leaped above gopher mounds and trails of ants
Feeling like I could fly.
Immersed in a Chagall landscape,
My father and I
Entered a place that held no fear or
Confusion or worry
Just dreams.
I stood atop a wooden
Bridge that groaned with the
Weeping willows,
Holding my arms out
Feeling wind, smelling dusty scents of hay.
Fish raced underneath, and
Dad grabbed a long stick, poking
Furry green masses of twigs,
A sea monster,
Held under the bridge as if trapped.
There were no voices, no sounds of
Loud trucks and whining wheels,
Just the sound of my little purple shoes
Descending the groaning bridge.

AS UGLY AS SIN

HOLON R.

The wise always puzzle forward.
Sure, that's true,
But, why do you move through life as if swimming in a sea of
    cement?
The wise always puzzle forward.

Black sheep of the family.
You are my father.
Unconditional love has always been, well,
Mutual.
The wise always puzzle forward.

The steady hand of a not-so-steady mother,
Shoving you
Towards a vast plane of nothingness.
The wise always puzzle forward.

Yeah, you could have gone
Far.
But you went the "high" road
More like getting high.
The wise always puzzle forward.

Marrying Mom,
One of the better decisions.
Yeah, it ended poorly.
But, doesn't everything?
The wise always puzzle forward.

Unconditional love is more
Your level.
That's something, I guess.
God, Dad, you may have screwed up
But, jeez, you are always there.

MOTHER

QUINN V.

If the world is listening, I want them to hear
The beeping monitors come alive.
A hand intertwined between pain medications
and a will to survive.
I want them to hear the hollowed-out thank you,
hidden behind a shallow breath.
I want the world to hear the water gliding across
the dishes ever so gently.
The swish of a broom picking up what has already
been forgotten.
I want them to hear the thank yous forgotten
I want the world to hear the crash of the forsaken
waves.
I want them to see the sea turtles encircling us.
I want them to know how grateful I am.
A mom, so special, unlike anyone else.
I want the world to know just how thankful
I am to call her mom.

MAN'S BEST FRIEND

BEN S.

They chose their path,
not their ancestors.
They chose to be tamed,
and teach us to be optimistic and loyal,
not their ancestors.
They come when named,
not like their ancestors.
But they can't lose the instinct
of their ancestors.

MAP OF THE STARS

ELYSE C.

If the world is listening
it should know
how a person
was crafted from the stars in the sky
and of a person
who changed the fate of many.

My uncle was beautiful
on the inside and out
even if others were blind to that.
His face dappled with freckles
like a map of the stars,
and fiery red hair,
all combed back with precision and care
and hiding behind
his thick round glasses
were two beautiful eyes,
filled with joy, laughter, and love.
His heart
challenged to keep up
with others around
and filled
with the eternal flame
of life
that had been burning from the beginning.

Downs was his friend
not his enemy.
And he was without a drop of sarcasm
or a bone with hate.
His downs made him who he was,
special,
and miraculous.

As a child he learned to care
for everyone and everything.
As a child he rode his bike
up the street and back down.
To everyone he met
he brought a smile,
but to his family he meant so much more.

THE AUNT I'VE ALWAYS WISHED FOR

LEDYSHA C.

The wise puzzle forward is my hero,
Ann Kenneth is her name
Mommy 2 is what we call her
a lady with short grape vine-like hair
and chocolate round eyes
a lady with a beautiful smile
that has the saddest stories hidden behind
a lady who struggled through many and still managed to stay
    standing.

She saved me with her love,
the kind of love that motivated me
the kind of love that secured my tears from falling
the kind of love that I could take wherever and whenever I go
the love that took my sadness and replaced it with my happiness.

The lady who has beauty that catches attention with her kind eyes
and catches the heart with her adoring personality
her smile mainly accomplishes her beauty when she greets,
her words speak and touch the heart with a mellow voice.

She is my hero, idol, and role model,
she advises and prepares me for the new coming life
she spoils me with her love,
she comforts me with a welcoming hug,
she brings laughter with her stories.

Ann Kenneth,
the one aunt I adore
the one aunt I look up to
and the one and only person that can bring joy to life
making joy happen with just one thing:
that is with a pinch of love and a simple smile.

MY MAMA AND I

Iris E.

The trapped giant we made small in our cupped palms,
Smiling down, we watched the giant shrink
From its lengthy height, as if insignificant,
My mama and I

I talked and she listened
I marveled at how all the aches and tears
Melted away at the warmth and strength
From the glow of my mama's sweet embrace

My mama took care of me, taking note
Of my triumphs and struggles, yet somehow
My mama taught me independence from the gray boundaries
Of a life without creativity or expression

So each morning when I wake to her soft brown eyes,
The first thing on my mind is my total and utter devotion
To my mama who has taught me:
To stand tall and flat on my feet,
How much capacity the heart can hold,
That I can do anything,
And the love that can be shown through
A single laugh,
or a word,
or even a giant we made small
Between our tightly clasped fingers,
My mama and I

STRENGTH

Hannah H.

If the world is listening I want them to know
of the fear that hung like a ghostly haze.
The dread of getting beaten,
Whipped,
Broken.

Every day was a struggle that could never be won.
but with his big glasses and chipped tooth
he carried on.
Raised himself and his siblings.

If the world is listening I want them to hear
the cries that echoed in the night.
The terror of when his stepfather came home.

The man would stumble in with the stench of alcohol in his
    breath,
looking for something to hit.

If the world is listening I want them to feel
the pride I feel today.
Knowing that my dad, after all the pain and sorrow,
after the war with sadness,
Fear,
Belts,
Bruises,
he emerged victorious.

If the world is listening I want them to feel his strength.

SHE WAS REALLY TOO YOUNG

Samantha M.

The trapped giant we made small
with so many stop signs she begins to fall.
She's only nine, yet
much more intelligent she is than I ever was at her age.

The hardships she faces,
she was really too young.
I fear for her when someone's to ask,
"What are your mother and father like?"
But, she won't ever know,
all because of the hardships she faced when she was too young.

The trapped giant we made small,
one day she will move on.
She will grow and learn to show she cares.
But, the hardships she faced when she was so small,
their chains of despair won't hold her down.
She will grow to be over ten feet tall.

CEREMONY

KAI C.

fire light whirled around the scene
the ninnescah's knife cut to the bone
two mangled hands clasped and shook
we were now brothers.

REFLECTIONS ON WRITING

I HAVE PROGRESSED in crafting poetry, and...learned that I really enjoy the art of writing poetry. I have come to realize and appreciate that writing includes brainstorming topics for a paper, collecting ideas for a story, jotting down random thoughts, and logging a journal entry. Writing brings me joy and peace, and lets my mind flow. It is exciting for me to know a variety of ways to express my feelings and give voice to my inner thoughts. I will definitely continue to write for pleasure and to develop further into a thoughtful, skilled writer.

—CATHERINE M.

WRITING WITH WILLIAM STAFFORD

ON MOMENTS IN TIME

THE WELL RISING

WILLIAM STAFFORD | *Composed 1953, Published 1960*

The well rising without sound,
the spring on a hillside,
the plowshare brimming through deep ground
everywhere in the field—

The sharp swallows in their swerve
flaring and hesitating
hunting for the final curve
coming closer and closer—

The swallow heart from wing beat to wing beat
counseling decision, decision:
thunderous examples. I place my feet
with care in such a world.

TRAVELING THROUGH THE DARK

WILLIAM STAFFORD | *Composed 1956, Published 1962*

Traveling through the dark I found a deer
dead on the edge of the Wilson River road.
It is usually best to roll them into the canyon:
that road is narrow; to swerve might make more dead.

By glow of the tail-light I stumbled back of the car
and stood by the heap, a doe, a recent killing;
she had stiffened already, almost cold.
I dragged her off; she was large in the belly.

My fingers touching her side brought me the reason—
her side was warm; her fawn lay there waiting,
alive, still, never to be born.
Beside that mountain road I hesitated.

The car aimed ahead its lowered parking lights;
under the hood purred the steady engine.
I stood in the glare of the warm exhaust turning red;
around our group I could hear the wilderness listen.

I thought hard for us all—my only swerving—,
then pushed her over the edge into the river.

REPRESENTING FAR PLACES

WILLIAM STAFFORD | *Composed 1956, Published 1962*

In the canoe wilderness branches wait for winter;
every leaf concentrates; a drop from the paddle falls.
Up through water at the dip of a falling leaf
to the sky's drop of light or the smell of another star
fish in the lake leap arcs of realization,
hard fins prying out from the dark below.

Often in society when the talk turns witty
you think of that place, and can't polarize at all:
it would be a kind of treason. The land fans in your head
canyon by canyon; steep roads diverge.
Representing far places you stand in the room,
all that you know merely a weight in the weather.

It is alright to be simply the way you have to be,
among contradictory ridges in some crescendo of knowing.

COMPASS ROSE

Julia R.

When you want something, close your mouth; when you want
    someone,
open your eyes.
Do not wait for the night hours
to come to you and whisper where to go from here. Grab the
    world until it coughs
and taste the dust motes that fall
from Heaven onto the floor of your bedroom.
Everything you waste your shooting stars on is only sitting in the
    shadows
waiting for you to cry out yes.
Yes.
Pay attention to the stories the world tattoos onto your fingertips
while you are too busy writing and erasing your own.
Decide what you would give up heaven for. Chase it
until your lungs bleed sunsets and dirt roads beat their whispers
onto the bare souls of your feet.
Run away, but run in circles
and hold your map tight in your teeth. Wait until the paper
    dissolves
and the roads blur and in that moment you know a new way to
    find home.

CEREMONY

Alex G.

The flowing Ninnescah of love was in the air.
She was covered in white.
The roots filled the seats and watched her float down the aisle.
He was quavering.
The deep blue sea stared into the dark brown woods.
She whispered "Forever" against the soft pink.

I KNOW WHO YOU ARE

Brielle B.

The staggering milestones convey a numerical distance that
    sustains me from you,
but I know who you are.

Years built the gates to our maturity, the grasp upon freedom as
    life guides us through the open air, yet
we both can now choose our own left our own right
but I still know who you are.

Once we clasped hands, our lips would form perfect matches,
    perfect forms, as we kissed leaving no room for anything
    between us, creating a time
where I knew exactly who you were.

A misfit turn, a bumpy and now caved-in corner I find myself in,
    but
I still look for who you are.

A solid blank page unravels into many wasted sheets, revealing
    the lost words of my remembrance
of who I hope you still are.

Planted in foundations of different kinds, we both sprouted, and
    opened into this place we called earth with purpose and little
    in common but one thing:
Love.
One thing I for sure know we both used to be.

But this unstable ground aches in fear, crumbling in the troubles,
    and you now find yourself in a place we know as the

war lands, but under heavy protection and layered arms,
from my ground I yearn to understand
who you are.

Once was then and the now has come. Knowing,
looking,
hoping,
yearning,
wondering,
being so sure of,
but forgetting.
And time erases.
Erasing the years we were strong, stubborn, and new like the
beginning life of a tree.
Side by side our roots grew deeper intertwining and interlocking
a grasp upon each other.
But growing up, growing out, apart and away, we look at the sun
from different beds now.
We watch the moons pass from different window seals and that
morning star that we once called ours doesn't seem to shine
the way it used to when we were younger.
Because at that point we both knew who each other was, and
thinking of you now, I still believe I know the person you
once were, somewhere inside you, still now.

But now as seasons change and I realize you have forgotten, I
understand, I no longer yearn, I no longer wonder, I already
know and I'm now sure of the fact
that it's you that no longer knows who I am.

MEMORY

ISABELLE M.

I stand before the deep canyon
of the dumpster.
The darkness of it spreading out before me,
devouring everything before it,
memories, left to rot by the dozen.
People would think about the things they had left behind.
These images would be coated in silver,
seeming much more special now that they were gone.
I lean forward.
The cold of the metal pressing against my bare arms.
My mind swerves, leaving me to hesitate.
Should I?
I glance back at my mom.
"Hustle, Isabelle," she calls.
"We have to go."
I turn and run my finger along her porcelain face one last time.
Her blonde hair floats gently around her forehead.
Her arms and legs flail as she falls.
The glowing moon glints off her icy eyes,
and for a moment I think,
she might spread her arms and fly back to me.
But it is too late.
She is just another memory.
I have pushed her over the edge.

CEREMONY

Selena L.-B.

The river is flowing
into me
as I settle into my new roots.
I shiver,
for some things
will forever be.

My Shavalas,
it's a good one
only I would say.
But my family won't stop
and my quavering won't stop.

ODE TO GOODNESS

KIAH B.

This is an ode to the process of forgiving
The pains of letting go
The vulnerable words leaving haunted like Halloween children
From lips that were once clenched in remorse.
This is an ode to the feeling of belonging
The handholds and pillow fights and skin against skin
In the middle of the night.
A crowd of 300 becoming one soul
Swaying to the sweet sound of Slow and Spun and
See You Again Soon.
This is an ode to moments of remembrances
The ones that are forced
And the ones that sneak up on you like snow days
The days that are tongue tied and unrequited and
Long.
Days where you could spend hours talking to the white wall in
    the kitchen
About everything and nothing
You felt silly but
He listened so well.
This is an ode to the good days and the bad
The toothpaste on the counter
Every time someone has held onto my shaking bones
And whispered lullabies that had nothing to do with nothing
And everything to do with everything.

This is my ode to goodness.

COURAGE

Karli G.

To tiptoe down Mom and Dad's staircase,
to walk on the balls of my feet to the desk
where my car keys rest,
to keep the keys silent by cupping my hands over them,
like holding a frog on a humid summer night,
to slowly unlock the front door,
softly—so my dog won't bark,
to look up into the starry, midnight sky
that holds the full moon,
to open my car door,
click the belt into place,
and drive away.

TEERAH

Annie L.

leaving
not looking back
the woods
thick at first
but thinning
as you
go on
you find one
that seems
perfect
but
as you climb
you find
it's quite menacing
you get
to the top
and decide to
jump
as you
prepare yourself
the wind
blows soft
yet you
shiver twice
once
for death
once
for success

LEMMINGS

Stuart S.

Cold days ahead
Mistake after mistake
History looks at us and laughs.

LITERARY DEVICES

Julia R.

I will say this without metaphor: poetry is not real
This poem is imaginary
unless
did it make someone hurt?
did it make someone feel?
did it make something real?
Do you whisper, zeugma, when you hand someone your ink and
    your heart?

Our pencils do not fit into the narrow alleys between our hearts
    and our bones and
we are all bruised in places that syntax and metaphor can never
    reach and never mend

These words are pointless because
it's not the rhythm of syllables but the staccato measures of our
    pulse
not where the lines end but our seams and scars
Enjambment: the moments that spill
helplessly into each other
the summers that trip into falls
the round the sun and back again until another repeat of the day
    you were born because
poetry is life is breath the lines share space we share the very
    breath that we question

The only real poem I ever wrote was to someone I loved
She had been hurt from beneath the skin the very insides of the
    hollow bird bones
I could not stop the reef of bruises from surfacing so I gathered
    the words I trailed and condensed them into something solid
nothing about the words mattered
they dissolved into reality with her tears and sublimated into
    ghosts of fog and apologies
They burst from the seeds of pain so something about them was
real after all

WHEN WAITING IS NOT ENOUGH

Catherine M.

At night, she floats downstairs to the living room,
Awakened by a presence hovering below lavender satin sheets
Ready to witness silent boxes perched on corners of mahogany.
Snooping, she learned early in life, was just like
Sticking your nose into a wine bottle with the cork on the edge
That flies across the table,
Surprising—much like when adults miraculously appear
Watching every step you take,
Acts of inquiry halted.
But the sky was dark, with stars that shone like glinting needle
    tips
Her Dörner piano tape winding
Notes slithering wheezily through walls,
Clinging to dusty paper and scraps of tea leaves
Warming her arms, casting a marmalade glow.
The crackling kept her awake at night,
Popping like an egg on a skillet that melts the eardrum
The egg full of panic, envious of its murderer who cracked its
    middle.
Reminding her of elementary school days
Anxiously watching popcorn bubble, spurting with buttery salt
Smelling it on her fingers as if it were yesterday.
Or her Grandma Clare's wooden sticks rolling out scarf after scarf
The sound perpetually ingrained throughout the house.
Yet still, she reaches towards the box
Ready to open the lid like an umbrella tempted by rain
Like jars full of passion ready to explode
As pillows do when they are plumped too much.
Reaching, she touches the clasp warmed from the fire,
And opens it.

REMEMBERING

JAIMIE G.

My memories are scattered across the country.
The people I'd grown to love
Hold out their hands
Asking to keep choice memories precious.
I gladly let people keep them.
But eventually
The friendships whither and gray,
Turning into shallow husks of what they once were.

As friendships fade,
So do the slices of memory.
I could go and gather up the remnants,
But when color returns,
It leaks outside the lines
Like a child playing with crayons.

Thinking of friendships that survived,
I smile.
The color in these memories triumph over the grey.

SATISFACTION

KIAH B.

It is in the last sentence of a paper you feel it.

The first tooth you lost
its slimy shine tied to a long piece of floss
dripped red as you presented it to your mother like a clean room
    or a 4.0.

The eve of your 14th birthday stung your tongue and fingertips
    with it
you're too old for things
but still so young.

It's the home before eleven
the first kiss outside of your white knobbed door
he lingered a little too long by your mouth
his nose kissed you before his lips did,
but you still felt it as he walked back to his car
you could still smell him on your
skin.

You're sitting in an audience
listening to a song sung by a girl whose thoughts are made of
    clouds
and your body is not your body anymore
so much so that when you lift your arm to dry soaking cheeks
you feel sorry for whoever's tears they are.
but they're yours
and they're beautiful.
She's singing the blues and she's your sister and you never want
to let go of this moment.
Like when you turned 14
or when he kissed you on your doorstep
or when you presented your tooth with arms stretched like
    innocence
or in that last sentence of a paper

and you felt it.

REFLECTIONS ON TEACHING WRITING

AS WE CELEBRATE the work and legacy of William Stafford, we celebrate his mindful attention to the individual moments of life, to the importance of those moments. In doing that, I believe we become better people, as well as better writers. When I was a young teacher, I remember him visiting an Oregon Council of Teachers of English conference at the coast. I knew I was in the presence of greatness, yet he could not have been more humble, more gracious to all of us. When I teach creative writing now, I hope, in some small way, to pass on his gifts of thoughtful wonder at the world around us and honest wrestling with ideas that matter.

—SARA SALVI, TEACHER

WRITING WITH WILLIAM STAFFORD
LESSON PLANS

The following pages contain unit and lesson plans designed by teachers who have worked closely with the William Stafford Archives at Lewis & Clark College. We hope you will use and adapt these plans in your own classroom or at your home writing desk. To make this easier for you, each page can be enlarged by 130 percent to reach standard letter size on a photocopier.

The William Stafford Archives, housed at Lewis & Clark College in Portland, Oregon, contain all the materials teachers and students will need to work with the lesson plans. You can reach the archives online at www.williamstaffordarchives.org

Thank you for keeping William Stafford's legacy as a teacher, a writer, and a believer in the revision process alive.

—Ooligan Press

NATURE AND THE WRITING PROCESS
Unit and Lesson Plans

Erin Fox Ocón

Objectives

* Discuss William Stafford's poetry
* Examine William Stafford's revision process
* Write new poetry based on William Stafford's poems
* Write about nature and how it is connected to thoughts and feelings

Basic Agenda

Each day will begin with a freewrite. Some days, the students may be completely free to choose their topic (there will be a student-generated list on the bulletin board of possible choices if they get stuck), while on other days they may write based on a prompt.

1) Background information or background vocabulary (if needed)

2) Read poem

3) Short presentation or discussion on Stafford's revision

4) Discussion questions / Student response time

5) Student poem writing time

6) Student poem sharing time

LESSON ONE: WILLIAM STAFFORD AND HIS WRITING PROCESS

To begin our unit on William Stafford, I divide the class into eight small groups. Each small group examines one paragraph of prose by William Stafford about writing and the writing process. I call these paragraphs Stafford's "writing advice."

Each group spends a class period reading the paragraph and preparing a brief presentation for the class, in which they summarize Stafford's thoughts and add their own thoughts on what he said. Each group makes a poster on butcher paper that can be displayed around the room to remind us of Stafford's words.

For four days in a row, two groups present at the start of class. While these groups present, the rest of the class takes notes on the presentations.

We constantly refer back to these notes throughout the Stafford unit and, at the unit's end, students write on the following prompt: *What William Stafford writing advice did you use throughout this unit? What William Stafford writing advice could you improve on?*

Agenda

1) Reintroduce freewrites. Discuss expectations of the prompt.

2) Freewrite time. The prompt will be "Poetry."

3) Share freewrites. Highlight vocabulary that may come up like "metaphor," "simile," "six senses of poetry." Or bring them up if they don't come up!

4) Who is William Stafford? Mini-lesson (power point/lecture).

5) Small groups examine William Stafford's writing advice. These are prose writings on his writing process. Each group will have about one paragraph to read and a set of questions to help prepare a short 2–3 minute presentation to the class. Each group will prepare a presentation that will be given

over the next few days in class. Teachers may want to have groups create posters or write notes on index cards.

Notes

This does not follow our basic lesson format, as it is the first day. As our days studying Stafford go on, two groups will present at the start of every class on the writing advice they read (so this will take a total of four class days).

Materials Needed

Handout I've typed of Writing Advice for each group (included on the next pages), cut into small sections for students to read. Blank note cards for students to write on, butcher paper for posters, or both.

PRESENTATION GROUP #1

"I don't believe that the most profitable way to become a writer is to seek intense experiences. If you write, things will occur to you. The activity of writing will make things occur to you in your mind. You write the documentary that you think, rather than the documentary that you live. When you write, it doesn't make so very much difference what you have done, or intend to do, but it makes quite a bit of difference what occurs to you at the moment you're writing."   —from William Stafford's "Five Footnotes
to *Traveling through the Dark*"

Key Vocabulary

DOCUMENTARY: Recreating an actual event. (This can be done through movies, TV, writing, music, etc.)

Key Thinking to Share with the Class

Does Stafford think you have to have lots of interesting and unique experiences in order to be a good writer?

What does he think you have to do to be a good writer?

How do you feel about this?

Anything else you want to share about this?

PRESENTATION GROUP #2

"The things that occur to you. You know, you start to tell someone
something. There are some things you think are more worth telling
than others. You get home and someone says, "What happened?"
You start to tell them. Sometimes you don't know why it is that
this seems important to you, but if you start to tell it, and then you
tell the things that make you feel a certain way about it, it begins
to be more. That's what writing is. You say something, and then
something else adds to it."

—from William Stafford's "Five Footnotes
to *Traveling through the Dark*"

Key Thinking to Share with the Class
What does Stafford think writing is?

*Do you agree with him that "there are some things you think are more
worth telling than others"?*

*Does Stafford think that you should just retell an event? What else
should you add to the event?*

Anything else you want to share about this?

PRESENTATION GROUP #3

"When I write, I like to have an interval before me when I am
not likely to be interrupted. For me, this means usually the early
morning, before others are awake. I get pen and paper, take a glance
out of the window (often it is dark out there), and wait. It is like
fishing. But I do not wait very long, for there is always a nibble—
and this is where receptivity comes in. To get started I will accept
anything that occurs to me."

—from William Stafford's "A Way of Writing"

Key Vocabulary
RECEPTIVITY: Being able to take in/listen to ideas and knowledge.

Key Points to Share with the Class
How does William Stafford write?

What is his metaphor for writing? How is writing like this?

How is this the same or different from how you already write?

Any other thoughts you want to share about this?

PRESENTATION GROUP #4

"Something always occurs, of course, to any of us. We can't keep from thinking. Maybe I have to settle for an immediate impression: it's cold, or hot, or dark, or bright, or in between! Or—well, the possibilities are endless. If I put down something, that thing will help the next thing come, and I'm off. If I let the process go on, things will occur to me that were not at all in my mind when I started. These things, odd or trivial as they may be, are somehow connected. And if I let them string out, surprising things will happen."

—from William Stafford's "A Way of Writing"

Key Vocabulary
TRIVIAL: Of little importance; ordinary, common.

Key Points to Share with the Class
If William Stafford thinks of something (in other words, if something occurs to him) does he always write it down?

Why does William Stafford write down even trivial things?

Do you already do this? Can you think of examples of times we've done this in class?

Any other thoughts you want to share about this?

PRESENTATION GROUP #5

"I must be willing to fail. If I am to keep on writing, I cannot bother to insist on high standards. I must get into action and not let anything stop me, or even slow me much…I am making something new, something that has not been judged before. Later others—and maybe I myself—will make judgments. Now, I am headlong to discover. Any distraction may harm the creating."

—from William Stafford's "A Way of Writing"

Key Vocabulary:

STANDARDS: A requirement that things are expected to live up to.
HEADLONG: Quickly, without stopping to think about it.

Key Points to Share with the Class

Does William Stafford have high standards for his freewrites? Why is this?

What would it look like if someone were "headlong to discover" when they were freewriting?

Will he go back and look at (judge) his writing later?

Any other thoughts you want to share about this?

PRESENTATION GROUP #6

"So, receptive, careless of failure, I spin out things on the page. And a wonderful freedom comes. If something occurs to me, it is all right to accept it. It has one justification: it occurs to me. No one else can guide me. I must follow my own weak, wandering, diffident impulses."

—from William Stafford's "A Way of Writing"

Key Vocabulary

JUSTIFICATION: Something that defends what you or someone else did. (Example: Her justification for lying was that she didn't want to hurt her friend's feelings.)

DIFFIDENT: Not confident; shy.

Key Points to Share with the Class
> *Describe how William Stafford writes.*
>
> *How does he defend his writing choices? Does he need to defend them?*
>
> *Does William Stafford think he has great impulses (ideas) of what to write?*
>
> *Any other thoughts you want to share about this?*

PRESENTATION GROUP #7

"Yet another attitude I find necessary: most of what I write, like most of what I say in casual conversation, will not amount to much...It will be like practice. In conversation I allow myself random remarks—in fact, as I recall, that is the way I learned to talk—so in writing I launch many expendable efforts."
>   —from William Stafford's "A Way of Writing"

Key Vocabulary
EXPENDABLE: Not worth keeping; okay to be sacrificed.

Key Points to Share with the Class
> *Does William Stafford use all of the material from his freewriting?*
>
> *If he doesn't use it all, why do you think he writes it?*
>
> *When have you done this in the past?*
>
> *Any other thoughts on this?*

PRESENTATION GROUP #8

"Writers may not be special—sensitive or talented in any usual sense. They are simply engaged in sustained use of a language skill we all have. Their "creations" come about through confident reliance on stray impulses that will, with trust, find occasional patterns that are satisfying."

—from William Stafford's "A Way of Writing"

Key Vocabulary

SUSTAINED: Over a long period of time.

RELIANCE: Dependence. (Example: Your dog has reliance on you to feed him every day.)

IMPULSES: Sudden urges that take place without a lot of thinking.

Key Points to Share with the Class

What does William Stafford think a writer is?

What does William Stafford think a writer should depend on?

How is this like or unlike what you have heard about writing in the past?

Any other thoughts on this?

LESSON TWO: "TRAVELING THROUGH THE DARK"

First freewrite prompts: choose one—dark, deer, roads, decisions.

1) Background vocabulary: what does it mean to swerve? Pair share—class share—write definition on board.

2) Read "Traveling through the Dark."

3) Look at first draft and final draft—in the first draft, he does not have the final line about pushing the deer. Why do you think he included this later? Why might he have not had it at first? Which version do you like better? Class discussion.

4) Discussion questions:
   - Craft—list the words he uses that help create the mood or that feel powerful to you. Share with group.
   - Content—why did Stafford make the decision that he did? Was it an easy decision for him? What decision would you have made?
   - Write in notebook. Share with group.

5) Student poem writing:
   - Show example of the poem teacher wrote in response (highlighting writing process).
   - Some choices that connect with "Traveling through the Dark":
     * A time you had to make a tough decision (possible starting line: I thought hard...)
     * A story you have that takes place in the dark (possible starting line:_____ through/in the dark...)
     * A story you have about a road or a roadside (possible starting line: Traveling through...)

＊ *Writing hints:* choose your words carefully to help create the mood. Build suspense about what happens at the end. Don't tell us the ending until the very last line.

6) Share student poems. Each student shares their end line with the class. Then, students who would like to can share their whole poem.

Note
Anticipated time period is 2 days (50 minute classes)

Materials Needed
Copies of "Traveling through the Dark"

LESSON THREE: "LEVEL LIGHT" AND "FALL WIND"

1) Background vocabulary: review meanings of compare and contrast. Today, we will compare and contrast two poems.

2) Read "Level Light" and "Fall Wind." Go over general meaning: what message does the light give Stafford? How does the fall wind make Stafford feel, and why?

3) Revision: look at rough draft of "Fall Wind" on the overhead. What do you notice about the first draft and the final draft? (It's much longer!) On overhead, highlight the words that stay from the first to the final draft.

4) Discussion Questions: in your small groups, compare and contrast the poems. Write down your ideas (can be done in a Venn diagram, or just simple lists). Go over similarities and differences as a class. If it doesn't come up, point out that both the poems show Stafford observing something in nature, and the event that he observes makes him feel/think something. Also, point out that the moods of the poems, while having similarities, are also very different (share with students the phrase "orange with its hope" from Stafford's daily write of "Level Light"). Is this normal? Can you feel one thing one day and another the next? Can both be true?

5) Student poem writing:
   - Show teacher examples.
   - Brainstorm on the following questions:
     * Think of a kind of weather or a time of day. What does this look like (especially the color)? What does it sound like? What does it smell like? How does it make you feel? What does it make you think of? Your answers can be hopeful, not hopeful, or mixed.
   - As students are brainstorming, have some pictures of

light/weather and clips of sound to help stimulate this process.

- Write a poem. Some possible starting lines:
  * Sometimes the _____; _____ crowds around the door.

6) Share poems. After writing poems and listening to poems, write, "How does your poem compare or contrast with Stafford's?"

Note
Anticipated time period is 2 class periods (50 minutes each)

Materials Needed
Copies of "Level Light" and "Fall Wind"

LESSON FOUR: "REPRESENTING FAR PLACES"

FREEWRITE: while we're in here, what is going on outside? So far, we've been looking at Stafford poems about things that happen right where we are—on roads not far from Hillsboro, or standing in our doorways. Now, we're going to start thinking a little bigger—to places that are farther away.

1) Background vocabulary: students divide into groups of six. Each student gets one word to define, illustrate, and use in a sentence. That will then be presented to their small group. After the small group presentations, we will review the words as a class.
   - Key vocabulary: WITTY, POLARIZE, TREASON, CONTRADICTORY, CRESCENDO, REPRESENTING

2) Read "Representing Far Places." Highlight the vocabulary they learned prior to reading this poem. How does this vocabulary help make meaning of the poem?

3) Give students typed copies of the first draft, along with the final draft. Highlight what stayed the same. Circle what's different. Then, write about how the poem changed/stayed the same as it was revised. Concentrate especially on the ending.

4) Discussion: share writing on poem revisions. How is the meaning of the first draft different from the meaning of the final? Share my theory that I think the more Stafford wrote, the more he was able to believe that it was okay to be simply the way he had to be. Do we often get the message that we have to be a certain way in social situations? Where do we get that message from? Go back to the first stanza. What feeling does that give you? How is this feeling related to the last two lines?

5) Student poem writing:
   - Share teacher example.
   - Choices: "The Way I Have to Be" or "What Far Place Do You Represent?"

6) Student volunteers share poems.

Note

This one may take 3 class periods

Materials Needed

Typed copies of first draft of "Representing Far Places" and copies of final draft of "Representing Far Places" (possibly on the same page as rough draft—side by side?)

LESSON FIVE: "THE VIEW FROM HERE"

1) Background Information: how many of you have seen movies about penguins? Here's just a short clip to show you what they do (*March of the Penguins* clip, or something similar).

2) Read "The View From Here."

3) Revision: show rough draft on the board. That day he wrote a lot on another topic (teacher load—that's how many classes and students teachers have to teach). He didn't use this for the poem, but maybe he just had to get it out in a freewrite, since it was something on his mind.

4) Discussion Questions:
   • Craft—what comparisons does Stafford make in his poem?
   • Content—how are the penguins and humans connected? What could be the cold that people feel?

5) Student poem writing:
   • Show teacher example.
   • Possible Prompts:
     * Pick an animal that is important to you. Describe that animal. How is it connected to people? Why is it important to you? What does it represent?
       Or, what far place do you think about (a place you've never been to)? Why is this place meaningful to you? How might it be connected to you?
       Or, describe a time you have been cold—either physically, emotionally, or both.

6) Student volunteers share their poems.

Note

This can be a one-day lesson

Materials Needed

Copies of "The View from Here"

LESSON SIX: REVISION

1) Students choose the poem that they are going to revise—
read poems to each other first and then write letters
recommending which poems they should revise.

2) Revision mini-lesson showing examples from William
Stafford poem (use "Representing Far Places" and the
revision handout). Class exercise: circle words you need to
look at more, write question marks next to lines you might
change.

3) Revision time; read revised draft to a partner.

4) Final draft writing time.

5) Read final draft aloud.

Note

Revision takes at least 2 class periods. Final draft poems can be
read aloud to the entire class or in small groups. Teachers may also
choose to use other publication methods (revision chart included
on next page).

REVISING

Word Choice: Make sure each word is as descriptive and as powerful as you can make it.	William Stafford changed the line in "The View from Here" from "the wind is always after them" to "the wind bites over them."
Length: See if there is anything you can take out from the poem. See if there is anything you can add to the poem.	Remember that William Stafford took out tons of lines from "Fall Wind." He only kept the really powerful lines and took off the lines that didn't fit as well.
Sensory Details: See if there are any sensory details that you can add.	In "Level Light," William Stafford uses the sense of sight to give lots of detail about color. In "Fall Wind," William Stafford uses the sense of hearing to add details about the sound of the wind.
Metaphors, similes, and personification: See if there are any places you can add these to make your poem more powerful.	William Stafford used personification in many poems, such as in "Level Light" when he says, "In one stride night then takes the hill." An example of a simile is in "The View From Here" where he says, "drooping their little shoulders like bottles, the penguins stand."

* Other tools that poets use that you might want to add include repeating sounds/words and rhyming.

Line length: Poetry lines should not be long. There should be about one idea on each line, or if there are more, they should connect in some way.

"Pods of summer crowd around the door;
I take them in the autumn of my hands."
—"Fall Wind"

Stanzas: Stanzas are like poetic paragraphs. A new stanza is begun by skipping a line. This usually means that you're going on to talk about a new main idea.

All of the William Stafford poems we've read are great examples of this. Look at them for more assistance.

Capitalization: Usually poets only capitalize the first word of the sentence, not the first word of every line.

"Traveling through the dark I found a deer dead on the edge of the Wilson River road."
—"Traveling through the Dark"

Punctuation: Use commas as you normally would: for instance, when you're listing items. Normally, poets have their end punctuation (periods, question marks, exclamation marks) fall at the end of a line.

"In Antarctica drooping their little shoulders like bottles the penguins stand, small,
sad, black—and the wind
bites hard over them."
—"The View From Here"

WRITING DOWN MY FAMILY
Using Oral Histories as Research
For Autobiographical Poems

ROBIN SCIALABBA

Unit Question

Where do oral family histories and autobiographical poetry meet?

Unit Goals

* Gain familiarity with the questioning and answering process.
* Engage members of their families in an interview to obtain information that will help them construct meaningful autobiographical poems.
* Use William Stafford's style, organization, and word choice in six of his poems to create their own original poetry.

Objectives

* Interview parent(s) to find more information about their families.
* Use interview responses and questions to infuse creative writing with relevant information, stories, and family anecdotes.
* Define and use active verbs, lively adjectives, and interesting nouns in autobiographical poetry.
* Analyze and discuss major themes in poems by William Stafford.
* Brainstorm, write, and revise original, autobiographical poetry.

Standards

* Increase word knowledge through systematic vocabulary development; determine the meaning of new words by applying knowledge of word origins, word relationships, and context clues; verify the meaning of new words; and use those new words accurately across the subject areas.
* Listen critically and respond appropriately across the subject areas.

* Demonstrate listening and reading comprehension of more complex literary texts through class and/or small group interpretive discussions.
* Evaluate the impact of word choice and figurative language on tone, mood, and theme.
* Revise drafts to improve the logic and coherence of the organization, controlling idea, the precision of word choice, and the tone by taking into consideration the audience, purpose, and formality of the context.
* Analyze how language and delivery affect the mood and tone of the oral communication and make an impact on the audience.
* Analyze the occasion and the interests of an audience, and choose effective verbal techniques and language to convey ideas.

Interview Guidelines
* Choose one parent to interview.
* Start with five urgent questions—ask about the things you want to know really badly but might not have been brave enough to speak about honestly before now.
* Conversations should yield several more questions and answers that build upon the original five urgent questions.

Transcription
* Students may use recording devices and tapes or CDs if they have them available to use at home. If they have a recorder on a cell phone, they may use that.
* Otherwise, they will handwrite their interview questions and responses and type the information they record in class.

On the Phone with Mom
* Objective: model the interview process for students by having them call my mom.
* Have students write one question before they meet her.

* Once she begins talking, have students prepare questions as she responds. They must listen carefully to her responses in order to do this. The best speakers are the best listeners: interrupting can disrupt the conversation.
* Their follow-up questions can:
  * Clarify confusion
  * Go into more depth and detail about the same topic
  * Formulate new questions about related topics

From the William Stafford Archives (Lewis and Clark College)

* Poems will be used for daily reading and writing activities, ideally as a springboard for students to think creatively about their lives.
  * "Parentage"
  * "Vocation"
  * "Listening"
  * "At Liberty School"
  * "In Fear and Valor"
  * "Thinking for Berky"

Time

* 8 lessons, each spanning approximately 1.5 hours per class meeting. Daily lessons may be spread out over a number of weeks, as desired.

Materials

* Class sets of the six poems and the discussion/writing prompts for each in chronological order
* Spiral notebooks for interviews
* InFocus Projector
* Document camera
* Master list of student usernames and passwords
* Treats for our poetry reading on the last day

Assessments: Formative and Summative

* Daily conferencing one-on-one
* Check-ins during the transcription process and the poetry workshops
* Presentation reflection
* Final interview, transcribed and typed
* All daily writing and reflection on the Stafford poems
* Three original drafts of poems
* One polished, revised poem that synthesizes the poetry study and the interview
* Daily discussion
* Final evaluation of the class
* Poetry revisions
* Poetry reading

DAILY LESSONS

⊘▸ DAY 1

* Share expectations: attendance, cycle grades, classroom conduct.
* Cover necessary materials for the unit (see list).
* Have students fill out information cards for contact and any urgent things I must know about them as students before we begin; collect these.
* Introduce the unit: part poetry reading and writing, part oral family history.
* Questions, concerns, comments.
* Cover interview and transcription requirements.
* The fun part:
* Prewrite for the interviews: ask five pressing questions for ONE member of your family who you still talk to.
    * Students write.
* Introduce sharing as an opportunity to learn things about each other and ourselves. Explain that silence is okay and that building trust takes time.
* Pass out packets of poems and prompts.
* Have InFocus set to William Stafford Archive: "Parentage."
* Introduce William Stafford:
    * Not a rapper.
    * Not a thug: actually a conscientious objector and a pacifist...define?
    * They will have two choices while reading his poetry: Reject him and make fun of him, check out, and avoid him; or listen to what he might have to say, and see how he can change their minds about inner struggles and life experiences.
* Share personal story about my dad...
    * Black sheep of the LAPD, not your average cop, not your average dad.

* Prewrite:
  * Who is your father: to you, to your family, to everyone else? Where does he belong? What is one thing you want from him?
* Share responses.
* Read "Parentage" aloud.
* Cover stanzas, line breaks, and repetition.
* Decipher Stafford's feelings about his father.
* Discuss: how are his feelings similar to/different from your own?

DAY 2

* Introduce questioning and answering process.
* Model interview process over speaker phone with Mom.
* Students practice recording.
* Debrief: frustrations: overcoming obstacles, other topics we could have developed during the interview, questions they wrote but didn't ask, questions that didn't get answered, problem-solving, how our written forms of the interview are different and how they're similar. Use document camera to make this transparent.
* Students add to their five questions from yesterday by anticipating answers and trying to develop the questions further—have at least fifteen by the end of today.
* Students will take their questions home, set up interview times with the designated family member, and be ready to transcribe by the following week—this leaves them the weekend to conduct their interviews. Offer to call parents to discuss the assignment. Allow for extra time with students who rarely see their parents.
* Transition into workshop: break for bathroom and fountain.
* Prewrite:
  * T-Chart—left side is Mom, right side is Dad.
  * Show them my T-Chart on the InFocus from the Powerpoint (have the slide ready).
* Students write, then we share.
* Read "Vocation": students highlight verbs and nouns.
* What did they notice about the verbs and nouns he used?
* Review verbs and nouns for use in their own poems.
* What could they take from this poem and put into theirs?
* What did Stafford say about his own parents?
* Were they happy?
* Remind them: transcription begins Wednesday!

⟲ DAY 3

* Begin with "Listening."
* Prewrite:
  * Five senses—review what the five senses are, have them choose one to describe one parent, explain why they chose the sense they did.
* Share.
* Write down all the words they can think of that describe that sense to someone else…give examples.
* Share.
* Read "Listening."
* Highlight all the verbs and nouns and any details that catch their attention.
* Share responses.
* How did Stafford's choice of words paint a picture in your mind?
* Begin composing a poem about that parent, using the words they chose earlier. Repeat that person's relationship (example: "My father…") in at least two stanzas.
* Transition into Friday's homework assignment:
  * Who did they chose to interview?
  * Why did they choose this person?
  * What are some anticipated difficulties with the process?
  * Three things they learned about their family member that they didn't know before…
* Logging in and getting Username/Password information distributed.
* Refer to format expectations from Day 1.
* Students spend time transcribing their interviews—computer time.
* Create a title and save work every 15 minutes!

⬭· DAY 4

* Prewrite:
    * What are the responsibilities of all parents to their families? How have yours succeeded? How have they failed with you?
* Loss: What are all the ways we can lose somebody? What are some of their experiences with loss? How has it impacted their lives? What are some good coping techniques?
* What happens with kids at school when they've experienced loss at home? How do other kids and teachers generally react? What are the warning signs that someone is coping with sadness?
* Introduce "At Liberty School" first: be careful to mention sensitivity with the topic. You can never know who is dealing with loss or who has survived. We must respect people's rights to be silent, and encourage those who need a space to feel safe sharing. Some people are more comfortable than others with speaking about their feelings. Some things people are currently going through will never be talked about or shared.
* Read "At Liberty School."
* Comprehension questions:
    * What happened at school?
    * Why was this girl important?
* Discuss: in a family, how can people heal?
* Transition to interview process:
    * Check in on their interview transcriptions: where are they in the typing process? What are their frustrations? Sudden realizations? Tips?
* Students transcribe.
* Save work!

⊙ᐧ Day 5

I may have students write multiple poems using their interviews. If this is the case, we'd replace steps 1–4 with printing interviews and conducting a poetry workshop around their work.

* Prewrite:
  * Tell your mom's story.
* Share.
* Introduce "In Fear and Valor"—background information.
* Read "In Fear and Valor."
* Students will highlight or underline all the symbols in the poem: share my example of the T-Chart after we've read the poem together. Have InFocus ready.
* T-chart (description and symbol with literal explanation).
* Compose poems: make a poem that exposes a mistake you made with your mom, or a mistake she made in her own life—this poem should tell the story of a big regret.
* What can we learn from our mistakes?
* Transition into transcribing.
* Reminder that they should be finished typing today: presentations on Friday.
* Cover oral presentation rubric and guidelines for cue cards: duration, presentation modes (eye contact, professional dress, etc.).
* Students work on computers.
* Save work!

DAY 6

* Review presentation guidelines.
* Make list of presentation order on the board—students volunteer the order.
* Have evaluation sheets ready for each presenter.
* Students write praise on a sticky note for each presenter: at least one thing they loved about the presenter's oral history. After each presentation, they'll give their notes to me on the evaluation sheet.
* Share oral histories.
* Assess learning.
* Transition into poem: brief break for bathroom and fountain.
* Prewrite:
  * How do you define home? What makes a place, a family, a home?
  * Describe your home and your favorite memory from there.
* Share.
* Discuss.
* How do you normally cope with being home for breaks?
  * What are some good alternatives to unhealthy ways of coping?
* Read "Thinking for Berky":
  * What does the narrator remember about Berky?
  * Describe your home and your favorite memory there.
  * Workshop a poem where you describe your reaction to and all your feelings about your home.
* Share poems.
* Dismiss for the weekend: safe, healthy decisions.

⊙ › DAY 7

* The next two days of the cycle will be spent picking apart your interviews for pearls of information to use in a poem.
* We'll reread, write, and revise to make at least one polished poem fit for publishing.
* Go back into your interviews.
* Highlight the interesting details and information—consider things the person shared that you didn't already know about them and find the stories in their responses. Consider using some of the questions you asked creatively for your poems.
* Prewrite a poem about the person you interviewed using the interview information and your own descriptions of them. Begin by describing them in single words: make a list.
* Dismiss.

⟳‣ DAY 8

* Students pick a first line from the Stafford list of unwritten first lines.
* Freewrite a poem about a sibling or a best friend.
* Share.
* Workshop interview poems from Friday: go back to the interview and the prewrite to continue writing.
* Share.
* Use an example of Stafford's revision process for the poem "Parentage" and read through his early drafts to track their changes.
* Describe Stafford's revision style: what does he do when he revises? What does he change? What do the changes mean? What do they add or take away from the original words? What can you take away from his revisions and use in your own writing process?
* Revise the poem.
* Type a polished draft.
* Reread the polished draft.
* Last-minute revisions of one poem. Remind them that Stafford would return to a poem over the course of many months.
* Poetry reading of revised poems: each student reads or I read their poems for them. Audience gives encouraging feedback.
* Talk about the poetry reading experience.
* Debrief the class.
* Assess the learning through a final evaluation/write-up.

Name: _____

Finish these phrases:

✳ In my opinion, poems are _____

because: _____

_____

✳ My favorite poem is _____

because: _____

_____

✳ The thing I like most about poetry is: _____

_____

✳ The thing I hate most about poetry is (and don't say "it's

boring" without explaining what you mean!): _____

_____

_____

✳ In order to write poetry, I need: _____

_____

_____

Fill in the blank with your feeling:

I _____ sharing and reading my writing aloud

because: _____

_____

WRITING DOWN MY FAMILY

Name: _____

Interview Guidelines
* Choose one parent to interview.
* Generate at least 15 questions that you could ask them.
* For each question, ask one follow-up question by anticipating their answers (you will have 30 questions at the end).

Parent's name: _____

Occupation: _____

Age: _____

In some families, it is considered rude to ask your parent when their birthday is, and sometimes parents "lie" about their age anyway. If this is true of your family, tell the story of "age" with the parent you chose for your interview: _____

_____

_____

_____

Why did you choose this parent? _____

_____

_____

_____

What will be difficult about sitting down to an interview with him/her? _____

_____

_____

_____

What will make this experience easier for both of you? _____

_____

_____

_____

_____

What does he/she need to know in order to be successful and give you everything you need to complete the assignment? _____

_____

_____

_____

_____

Favorite meal: _____

_____

Favorite saying or quote: _____

_____

_____

_____

Happiest memory: _____

_____

_____

_____

Biggest regret: _____

_____

_____

_____

Biggest fear: _____

_____

_____

_____

Deepest worry: _____

_____

_____

_____

Biggest victory/success/accomplishment: _____

_____

_____

_____

Definition of love: _____

_____

_____

_____

Definition of family:_____

_____

_____

_____

Responsibilities of parents: _____

_____

_____

_____

Responsibilities of children: _____

_____

_____

_____

Greatest hope/wish:_____

_____

_____

_____

Interview Questions

* Write the answers carefully—if you have a cell phone, you can record the conversation with your phone so you don't lose it in the writing process.
* You may use ANY technology that will help you with this project!
* Avoid questions that elicit one word (or dead-end) responses.
* Ask questions to find answers for who, what, when, where, and why.
* Set up a time to meet with your parents and keep this commitment!

1. _____

_____

_____

Follow up: _____

_____

2. _____

_____

_____

Follow up: _____

_____

3. _____

_____

_____

Follow up: _____

_____

4. _____

_____

_____

Follow up: _____

_____

5. _____

_____

_____

Follow up: _____

_____

6. _____

_____

_____

Follow up _____

_____

7. _____

_____

_____

Follow up: _____

_____

8. _____

_____

_____

Follow up: _____

_____

9. _____

_____

_____

Follow up: _____

_____

10. _____

_____

_____

Follow up: _____

_____

11._____

_____

_____

Follow up: _____

_____

12._____

_____

_____

Follow up: _____

_____

13._____

_____

_____

Follow up: _____

_____

14._____

_____

_____

Follow up: _____

_____

15._____

_____

_____

Follow up: _____

_____

WRITING DOWN MY FAMILY

Name: _____

Attach your poem to this sheet
This is a collection of unfinished first lines William Stafford wrote as notes but didn't use as poems.

Directions
Use one of the following William Stafford lines as the first line for a poem about your family:

Sound is beginning to burn...

Put alone where no one can live...

My father and my mother have gone...

Where water lives long enough to ghost the land...

When rain hits our house...

The dog that ran across our yard...

If the world is listening...

All secrets added make the answer, coming near...

The wise always puzzle forward...

Sometimes what your part of the world gives...

The trapped giant we made small...

Finding you took all this time...

Some people, they say, turn to each other...

Tips:
- ✳ DON'T try to finish Stafford's poem FOR him.
- ✳ DON'T try to figure out what HE meant.
- ✳ DO figure out what you want his phrase to mean for YOU.
- ✳ DO find a way to make his line relate to YOUR family.
- ✳ DO use his line as a springboard for YOUR own ideas and images.
- ✳ IF YOU GET STUCK…START WRITING! Even if what you write is nonsense, if it gets your mind working and your hand moving, it's useful and helpful.

Questions to make you think before you write your poem:

Which line do you like best?_____

_____

_____

_____

How does this line relate to your family? _____

_____

_____

_____

What kinds of other details could you add to your poem to make it fit with the line from William Stafford? _____

_____

_____

_____

Will your poem be about your WHOLE family or just one specific member? Explain: _____

_____

_____

OOLIGAN PRESS ACKNOWLEDGMENTS

Ooligan Press is a general trade publisher rooted in the rich literary tradition of the Pacific Northwest. A region widely recognized for its unique and innovative sensibilities, this small corner of America is one of the most diverse in the United States, comprising urban centers, small towns, and wilderness areas. Its residents range from ranchers, loggers, and small business owners to scientists, inventors, and corporate executives. From this wealth of culture, Ooligan Press aspires to discover works that reflect the values and attitudes that inspire so many to call the Northwest their home.

Founded in 2001, Ooligan is a teaching press dedicated to the art and craft of publishing. Affiliated with Portland State University, the press is staffed by students pursuing master's degrees in an apprenticeship program under the guidance of a core faculty of publishing professionals.

Project Managers
Laura Larrabee
Rachel Pass
Rebecca Stevens
Michael Berliner

Editing
Jennifer Tibbett
Amreen Ukani
Sarah Currin-Moles

Cover Design
Lorna Nakell

Interior Design
Adam Salazar

Advisory Board
Abbey Gaterud
Tina Morgan
Whitney Smyth
Jonathan Stark

Marketing
Laurel Boruck, Keely Burkey,
Adam Salazar, Annie Whitcomb,
Meaghan Corwin, Margo Pecha,
Lauren Brooke Horn, Kelle Riley
Melissa Gifford, Ariana Vives,
Geoff Wallace, Zach Eggemeyer,
Lauren Hudgins, and Lacey Friedly

COLOPHON

We Belong in History is set in Apollo MT Std, Futura Std, and Trend Slab. It was designed with students, teachers, and poets in mind.